Rolling Out
Your Project

Other books by Sarah W. Fraser

Accelerating the Spread of Good Practice: a workbook for health care

The Patient's Journey: mapping, analysing and improving health care processes

Rolling Out Your Project

35 tools for
healthcare improvers

Sarah W. Fraser

Kingsham

First published in 2002
by Kingsham Press

Oldbury Complex
Marsh Lane
Easthampnett
Chichester, West Sussex
PO18 OJW
United Kingdom

Typeset in AGaramond
by Marie Doherty

Printed and bound by
MPG Books
Bodmin
Cornwall
United Kingdom

ISBN : 1-904235-08-5

British Library Cataloging in Publication Data
A catalogue record of this book is available from the British Library

Fraser, Sarah.

About the author

Sarah W. Fraser is a Visiting Professor at the University of Middlesex and an Independent Consultant. She has had a number of operational and management roles in both the private and public sector including Esso/Exxon and the NHS. Her area of expertise and consultancy at national and international level focuses on improving performance through developing leadership and organisational capability. She uses quality improvement methodologies as well as insights from systems thinking and the complexity sciences.

Contents

Introduction

Large variation across health care organisations, teams and individuals is no longer acceptable. Initiatives in the UK National Health Service (NHS) to reduce variation and improve the delivery of services to patients and users include a number of wide ranging structural changes, such as the introduction of the Commission for Health Improvement, National Institute for Clinical Effectiveness, as well as clinical governance requirements in organisations.

Other more interventional initiatives include nationally targeted improvement projects such as the Primary Care Collaborative, Cancer Collaborative, National Booked Admissions Programme, Coronary Heart Disease Programme and the Medicines Management Services Programme.

In a process intended to reduce variation and make benefits widely available, the above NHS projects all include a phase where innovations and improvements developed in one primary care practice or hospital are rolled out to other similar teams and organisations. The intention of these programmes of change is to take these 'pilot' improved systems, and implement these in other organisations across the NHS.

The spread and adoption of existing practices is a difficult and complex process. Much of the research on how this process works has focused on how one innovation has spread to many locations. Whilst there is some relevance from these studies for large scale spread programmes, they may not reflect the complexity of multiple innovations and their inter-relationships, or the local contextual differences between individuals, teams and organisations.

This guide provides a number of tools and resources for project managers and facilitators whose duties cover the rolling out of pilot projects to other teams and organisations. It does not attempt to provide a specific framework for a rollout project. Instead, the tools are designed to give the user sufficient insight so that they can develop a bespoke programme that specifically takes into account the characteristics of the subject matter and the local context.

It is recommended that you start by analysing your pilot project to make sure you understand its intricacies and nuances. Then spend time working out and understanding the potential new users you are targeting, including assessing their readiness for change. This is important in helping you prioritise your activities.

Next you need to consider how this rollout process will become part of the everyday fabric of the new organisations and teams that you hope will take on the new practice – this is called mainstreaming. Finally, there are some tools to help you work through a rollout planning process as well as hints and tips to ensure sustainability of your efforts.

If you're a newly appointed project manager you will find this guide a valuable resource to build your understanding and capabilities for rolling out your project. Other leaders can use the tools to steer their thinking and guidance to their staff. Each section starts with a story about Heather and Richard's experiences as project leaders, then there is a description of each tool and when it is best used. The tools follow this description and they are designed to help your thinking process and can be used as project team meeting agenda items for discussion.

Section A

Analysing the pilot project

Richard and Heather have both been recruited to join a national programme of change. There has already been a project to develop innovative solutions for the management of patients with diabetes and now their role is to spread these results across a wide variety of teams and organisations.

"I don't know much about diabetes", declared Richard. "Being brought in at the last minute means I don't have the experience and knowledge that you have."

Heather looked up from the project management manual she'd been reading, "Just because I'm a nurse and was involved in the pilot project, doesn't mean I know how to roll it out to others. In fact, it's difficult for me to remember just how tricky it was to design and implement the new ways of working."

"Do you think I need to know about diabetes to be able to do my job?", said Richard.

"I think you'll need to be able to explain the solutions we came up with", replied Heather.

"Well, I've just visited Mainroad hospital and to be honest it was difficult to identify the new ways of working. It all seemed very organised."

"That's just the point – it was totally frenetic before we made the changes. Patients were wandering all over the place, notes were lost, there was a high rate of sickness amongst the staff. A real mess. The changes should be obvious"

Richard frowned. "They might be obvious to you, but to me they're not. I doubt they would be to any of the doctors, nurses and managers that I will be working with. How about you spend some time with me at Mainroad explaining just what does need to be spread to other places"

Heather sighed. "OK, but only if you help me later with the project management plans."

When they arrived at Mainroad Hospital, Heather was overwhelmed with greetings and hugs from most of the staff. Richard felt very much like a spare part and waited in the background until the fuss died down.

"I don't think I'll ever be able to part with this project," said Heather, "after spending eighteen months going through the mill together we really bonded."

Richard made a mental note of thanks that he hadn't been so deeply involved in the pilot. How else could he spread the results to others if he couldn't give up spending time with it?

"Heather, can you take me through just what it is we're supposed to be rolling out to others?"

"OK, let's start with the specialist nurse. You see, she has a number of new roles."

"No, I don't see her new roles. Can you show me please", said Richard, getting more impatient.

"How can I show you roles? They just happen. Oh, I suppose I could give you her new job description."

"Well that's a help for a start. Does it show her relationship with others? What about the clinical decisions? Is there a written pathway or something I can take away with me?"

Heather felt Richard was being very demanding and unappreciative of what the changes were about. "When we introduced the new ways of working we didn't spend all our time writing things up, we just did it. We're not managers you know."

Richard bit his tongue. "Perhaps you can walk me through the process as if I were a patient."

"Fine. You'll see some of the changes doing it that way, though it's going to be very difficult to explain the detail."

"Did you make the changes in a certain order? Were some dependent on other things? Did it all happen in a nice linear fashion or did you do it piecemeal?

"Why do you need to know all that? I thought you just wanted to know about WHAT we came up with in the end," queried Heather.

"If I have an idea about the process you went through it might help me understand how all the pieces of the pilot project fit together. In turn that might help me see where to start in my rollout project."

Heather and Richard spent the afternoon walking through the new ways of working, with Heather doing her best to describe to him both the process they went through and the outcome that is now in place. Richard took lots of notes.

Analysing your pilot project; some introductory thoughts

What is the "good practice"?

In healthcare we are not short of good ideas. Good practice exists everywhere and there is constant creativity as individuals adapt and change according to their local circumstances. There are few if any roles in healthcare that do not form part of larger teams. Many professionals, managers and administrative staff may belong to a number of very different teams and groups, and boundaries between these groups and organisations are often unclear.

What does this have to do with rolling out projects and spreading good practice? Well, the complexity of the relationships between individuals makes it difficult to both make the good practice explicit and to help new behaviours be adopted. What may at first seem like a simple idea can turn out to be quite complicated.

For example, an orthopaedic consultant may take his diary with him to his clinic and give the patient a date for the next appointment whilst they are in the room. This may help reduce waiting times and most patients will appreciate the opportunity to agree the date and time of their next appointment. However, this 'simple' idea is a fairly complex system of concepts and practices that has different component parts. To scale up this good idea across all orthopaedic consultants, all clinics, the whole hospital and perhaps to other hospitals is not an easy process and will demand insights into what are the ideas behind the perceived good practice.

Challenges in understanding good practice

If you are planning to develop a programme to support the roll-out of a pilot project then you will already have some idea of what it is you want to encourage others to adopt. Much of the literature on the diffusion of innovations tends to look at how one innovation, and usually a simple one, is adopted by others. The research seldom takes into account that many innovations, sets of good practice that leaders wish to spread, are in fact made up of very complex behaviours and interactions. Also, the target audience of new users tend to experience a number of innovations and new ideas competing, at the same time, for their limited attention.

Add to this the fact that much of our knowledge is tacit. This means it is not something we notice or can easily describe – we just know it. If you have experienced teaching someone to drive a car then you will have experienced trying to make your tacit knowledge explicit. This is not an easy task. Similarly, it is difficult to make explicit the good practices within a pilot project.

Taking the first step

If your role is to enable and support others through the process of adopting existing good ideas from a pilot project, then the very first step is for you to learn about what it is you are trying to encourage others to adopt. If what you are planning to spread is complex, then you will need to work out what is not included in your rollout plans, reduce the system to its component parts, assess their interrelationships and identify the underlying ideas and concepts for each part. With this knowledge you can then assess the preconditions for adoption. These are the factors that can help accelerate the adoption process and reduce resistance to change. Finally, there are ways you can describe your ideas that will help adopters understand them.

Throughout this guide, the word 'system' will be used to represent the good ideas, behaviours and practices that you are intending to help spread. There is no right or wrong way to identify the parts of the system. Different project leaders may define the same system differently. This is fine. The most important aspect of this step is to spend some time working out how you can describe the parts of the system to others.

This section covers the following issues:

1: Working out what is included

Your starting point is to define the system that your pilot project covers. This includes working out what is not included in your rollout project.

2: Identifying component parts of the system

Here you are shown how to divide your improved system into smaller and more manageable parts. If you find it very difficult to identify the component parts then it could be that the system is very complex. Complicated systems are more difficult for adopters to understand so this may be your first indication of the need to find some ways to divide the system into smaller 'bite size' pieces for the adopters. Break it down and then see if you can find even smaller parts.

"Testing out something new that is small, manageable and if it doesn't work, can be stopped, is helpful for reducing the resistance to change."

The more you can reduce the system of ideas to manageable pieces, the more likely potential adopters will have a go at implementing them. This is particularly so for healthcare where staff may be more risk averse (and there's nothing wrong with that) that means many professionals are cautious adopters. Testing out something new that is small, manageable and if it doesn't work, can be stopped, is helpful for reducing the resistance to change.

The next two tools are important. We know from research and from practice that in most cases it is the ideas and concepts behind the 'good practice' that trigger the attention of adopters. Pushing detailed solutions onto potential adopters may actually increase their resistance to change. This is because they have difficulty in seeing how someone else's solution will fit in their local circumstances.

> *"Pushing detailed solutions onto potential adopters may actually increase their resistance to change."*

This is a particular issue for pilot project where the results have attracted the attention of leaders who wish others to achieve the same benefits. Not understanding, that different contexts play a very important role in the ability to adopt similar practices and to get similar results, will hinder the change process.

3: Differentiating the 'what' from the impact

This is an analysis that helps you see the difference between the solutions that you may have identified as worthy of spreading to others, and the impact of those solutions. Impact is the ultimate aim of encouraging the spread of good practice and focusing on this is a useful way to focus adopters on the opportunities and benefits of testing and taking on something new.

4: Identifying key concepts

In the same way Tool 3 helps you see the wider implications, and the perhaps more conceptual level of the system you wish to help spread, Tool 4 assists you in discovering the key concepts underlying the pilot project.

The first four tools in this chapter aim to help you through the process of understanding the 'what' it is you are helping to spread. By working through them you will gain some insight into the system and also how to develop a 'script' that you can start using with potential adopters now.

Systems are complex and continually adapt and change over time. It is neither possible nor pragmatic to carry out an analysis that reflects the details and dynamics of your system. Instead, this chapter leads you through ways in which you can start to develop your thinking and understanding. The following four tools gain some insight into how the different parts of the system interrelate. These are only the start. As you learn more about what it is you are encouraging to spread you will discover more about how different parts are connected and related, and how they influence each other. Analysis doesn't take away the need for testing out and learning from real life. Use these tools to get ideas, and then engage with potential adopters of your system

5: Identifying independent components
6: Identifying dependencies
7: Supporting action

These are tools that aim to get you thinking about where you might start and which areas need to wait until other actions have been taken. The output from these analyses will provide you with an indication of the possible 'early wins' whilst also suggesting what might be the timescales for the whole initiative, once you've taken dependencies into account.

As complicated systems have so many parts, it is useful to know not only where to start implementing changes and gaining quick successes, but also to understand what other activities you need to do to prepare the ground for adopters to be able to adapt to new ways of working. Time passes quickly. Starting work on the longer-term aspects helps accelerate the whole process of change.

If you have worked through Tools 1 to 7 you will have a sketchy but useful idea of just how complicated your set of ideas for spreading are. You may have reached this stage in a short time, speeding through the tasks relatively easily.

If you have struggled in the analysis of your system and found it difficult to describe the pilot project and its good practices then you have experienced some of the difficulties potential adopters may have. Much of what you would like to see spread is knowledge and experience that is tacit; it is not obvious or easily visible. The tasks you have completed so far are designed to stimulate your thinking, arouse your curiosity and elicit some of this tacit knowledge.

8: Preconditions for change

The final steps in understanding good practice involve you assessing the preconditions required for adoption of each part of your system.

9: Describing the pilot project

The final tool in this chapter is designed to help you describe your pilot project in a way that helps the target adopters understand the good practice so they can decide whether to adopt the changes or not.

Having completed the tasks covered in the next few pages, the following chapter will focus on ways to target your potential new users in an efficient way. If you have completed most of the analyses in this chapter you will already have a wealth of information to assist you in the next stage of developing a programme to roll out your pilot project.

Tool 1: Working out what is included

Objectives:

- Describe the scope of the system
- Assess what is *not* included in your project

Task:

a) Write a narrative description of the system

b) List any limitations or areas that you feel are not included in the system
   (for example, changing the hospital wide scheduling system may not be your first priority if you are encouraging the adoption by consultants of ways of giving patients appointment dates at the time of the clinical decision)

Hints and tips:

- Narrative writing, instead of using bullet point summaries, is a useful way to gain insight into the wider system of practice
- Starting with what is not included may be helpful in defining the system
- Ask the source of the good ideas to describe what they do and what they think is excluded
- Start writing something, you can always come back and refine it later!

Tool 2: Identifying component parts of the system

Objectives:

- Describe at least one way of viewing the 'pieces' of the system
- Prepare for further analysis of the relationships between each piece and the pre-conditions for adoption

Task:

Divide the system into at least 5 different parts.
Name these parts and give a little bit of description to each one.
You may wish to start a table like the one shown below as this can be used for the basis of some of the other tools in this part of the workbook.

	1	2	3	4	5
Name					
Description					

In the booked admissions example we could have the following component parts
- *Patient's diary*
- *Consultant's diary and booking system*
- *Process at the clinic*
- *Confirmation process*
- *Follow up and feedback (e.g. if patient doesn't attend next time)*

Hints and tips

- One of the easiest ways is to start with the flow of people or information
- Try and find at least 5 parts. Go up to 7 or 8 if you like but any higher and your analysis may become unwieldy
- You may find someone else has written up the system; this would be a good source for this step, though you may like to customise it to suit your local circumstances
- This exercise is not specifically about looking at the process or pathway. You could use this as your basis for analysis, though you may get other insights if you think a little more laterally

Tool 3: Differentiating the 'what' from the impact

Objective:

- Separate solution from impact

Task:

Complete the matrix below.
Under *solution*, note the key features that seem to be important in the source system.
Under *impact*, relate these features to the wider improvement goals, noting how they achieve individual, team or organisational aims and any impact that the patient may perceive.

Solution	Impact
For example • *Consultant updates his diary during the clinic* • *Patient negotiates and agrees the next appointment date and time during the clinic*	*For example* • *Less duplication and potential for error in the administrative systems* • *Patient more satisfied, less anxious waiting for a letter giving a time, has actually agreed when to come and will probably turn up as agreed*

Hints and tips:

- It is often difficult for the source of good ideas to see the wider impact; if you are the source, then you may like to ask someone else to help you understand and explain the impact of what you are doing
- Start writing something; you can always come back later and refine your thoughts!

Tool 4: Identifying key concepts

Objectives:

- Identify the principles underpinning the good practice
- Develop the ability to explain the system to others without mentioning the detail of the solution

Task:

Focus on the system, take a step back and make notes about what is happening, without mentioning any detail of the solution.

For example, the patient is being involved in the decision-making process, saving elapsed and actual time, avoiding duplication and error, enhancing relationships between doctor and patient.

Hints and tips:

- This is easier to do if you have already completed Tools 1, 2 and 3
- Concepts are often linked to wider aims and goals; e.g. to reduce wastage, so check the ideas you generated under 'impact' in Tool 3
- Write down just verbs such as – coordinates, reviews, communicates etc.
- Capture your thoughts in short phrases rather than long descriptions

Tool 5: Identifying independent components

Objectives:

- Identify parts of the system that can be implemented without needing other parts of the system to be changed first
- Discover points of leverage to help adopters at least try something manageable

Task:

a) Working with the components you identified in Tool 2, note down those that can be implemented independent of any other part of the system.

For example, the confirmation process in the orthopaedic clinic can get through a process of improvement and change without the whole of a booked admissions process being implemented; e.g. new letters or postcards can be designed.

b) Then brainstorm and list some of the small actions that an individual can take, the ways they can change their behaviour so they implement the independent parts of the system.

Hints and tips:

- If you initially divided your system into component parts at a high strategic level, you may find it useful just to do the brainstorming task
- If you know of someone who has adopted your system or a component of it, then ask them where they began, and why they chose that piece to start with.

Tool 6: Identifying dependencies

Objectives:

- Identify parts of the system that need to be implemented before others can be actioned
- Identify key constraints to implementing the system as a whole

Task:

Working with the components you identified in Tool 2, note down those that cannot be implemented without something else being in place. Note down what is dependent on what.

This can't be implemented...	Before this...

Hints and tips:

- Don't worry about the level of detail. If you think there might be a dependency, no matter how large or small, then note it down
- If you know of someone who had adopted your system or a component of it, then ask them what dependencies and constraints they encountered.

Tool 7: Supporting action

Objectives:

- List some key starting points
- Identify what you can do to speed up actions required for contingent parts to start

Task:

Make notes on how you can encourage the adoption of independent parts.
Also think through and make notes on what actions you can take now or need to include in your strategy to work with dependencies.

Parts, ideas to spread...	Actions to take...
Easy stuff to start with: • • • • •	
Things that need to be put in place for the successful adoption of the whole system: • • • • •	

Hints and tips:

- Capture your early thoughts now, you can firm up your actions later
- This is an important prioritisation process. You only need a few activities to get started and it's best not to start with those that will be very difficult to complete. It's ok to go for the simple, easy tasks first!

Tool 8: Preconditions for change

Objectives:

- Identify what circumstances will help adopters take on parts or the whole of the new system
- Discover circumstances that seem to help the change process that you can build on (this is in contrast to focusing on the barriers and trying to overcome them)

Task:

Make some notes under the following headings about what you would look for before starting to implement any changes in a team or organisation:

Leadership:

People:

Policies:

Resources:

Hints and tips:

- Be specific to your identified good practice and avoid generalisations about change.
- Investigate what helped the pilot project to work
- Match some of the dependencies from Tool 6 to the various enablers that will help you to overcome them
- Think and write positively. Focus on what will help make it happen, not what will stop change happening!

Tool 9: Describing the pilot project

Objective:

- Describe the improved system in a way that encourages others to adopt new ways of working

Task:

Answer the following questions, briefly. If you find this difficult, then you may need to learn more about the good practice (Tools 1 to 7).

How much is this new way of working better than the current practice?

How closely does this reflect the beliefs and values of the potential adopters?

How easy is it to try out the new way?

How readily can the old way be re-instituted?

How easily can the new ways of working be described to others? Is it visible in any way?

Hints and tips:

- These questions form the beginning of the 'script' you can use to influence new users. Make short bullet point note now; you may like to return to this tool and write it up in more detail at a later stage.
- If you want to learn more about these questions, then you can read about them in a book by E. Rogers, "The Diffusion of Innovations", The Free Press: USA. 1995

Section B

Assessing readiness for change

Richard had spent the past week in his office gathering information about the seven organisations to whom he was supposed to be rolling out the diabetes project. In contrast, Heather spent the week with one organisation, walking the corridors, meeting people (some of whom had nothing to do with the project) and discussing the latest diabetes audit with the specialist nurse.

"No wonder you're stressed," said Richard, "spending a whole week in one organisation is a luxury that I couldn't' afford. By the time you've visited them all you're supposed to have started to implement some changes"

"I know," cried Heather, "but how else can I work out who to start with?"

"I think you're getting into too much detail. Like me you've got seven organisations to work with. Surely you need to start by assessing which is the best one to start with?"

"How can you assess an organisation when you don't yet know the people, policies and culture?"

Richard walked over to his bookshelf and pulled out three books that he had used when studying for his MBA. "There are a number of analytical techniques you can use, like culture questionnaires," he said, leaving the books on the table in front of Heather.

Ignoring the books, Heather said, "That's all very well, but I prefer to find out about the people, who they talk to, what they talk about, why they do what they do."

Richard laughed. "Sounds like you should be doing a psychology degree!".

"Well, it's eventually individuals who need to change and organisations are just collections of individuals. I'm going to stick with my strategy of finding out about the key people. Though I'll spend only a couple of days at each hospital. Will you stick with your questionnaires?"

Just then their office door opened and Cathy, the programme director to whom both Heather and Richard reported burst into their office. "Hi guys, how's progress?"

"We're discussing how best to go about targeting the places where we need to rollout the project," explained Richard.

Cathy frowned. "What are you doing that for? The strategy plan shows you where you need to be working and with whom. The focus now is on getting the new diabetes services implemented as soon as possible."

"We know that," said Richard, "but we're trying to prioritise our efforts."

"We can't work with all the organisations at the same time," implored Heather.

Cathy stepped up to the large Gantt chart on the wall. This showed the organisations and the times when Richard and Heather should be working with them over the next two years. "This tells you what you should be doing."

"That's all very well, but that is just a planning tool for convenience," explained Richard. "We're interested in whether the organisations are ready to change yet."

"I would prefer to work with someone who wanted to change, than push myself on them," said Heather. "I've just spent some time with Upperway hospital and they don't seem ready to change at all. I think that forcing them right now wouldn't be a constructive process."

Cathy, taken aback, enquired, "Are you suggesting my initial plan is wrong?"

"No," said Heather, "we're just seeing it as a strategic direction. What we're interested in doing now is turning it into a plan for action."

"And we want to base it around some analysis of readiness for change so we can target our efforts most effectively," explained Richard.

"OK, I see what you mean," said Cathy, walking to the door. "How are you doing the analysis and assessment?"

Richard and Heather looked at each other. "We were just discussing that when you came in. We haven't finalised it yet," said Richard.

"Fine. Let me have your actions plans by the end of the week," said Cathy as she left the room.

Assessing readiness for change: some introductory thoughts

Before the launch of a new product on the market, companies will undertake a programme of planning and market research. The research and development phase for the product will have included work on which sector of the market will be targeted.

In social systems we can have social products and these can benefit from social marketing techniques. So, even if your product is not going to be 'sold', you still need to define your target adopters and assess their readiness for change. By understanding their motivations and incentives to change, you can plan your activities to achieve maximum impact.

In this chapter there are a variety of tools all designed to help you improve your understanding of the individuals, teams and organisations that you would like to adopt the working practices developed in your pilot project.

10: Drivers for change

Every team and organisation will have its own set of criteria and reason for change. Their working context, although similar to others, will be unique. You can use this tool at a high level to assess the reasons for change for all organisations. However, you might find it useful to carry out this short analysis for each organisation you will be working with. Pay attention to the difference and explore why it is you think there are different motivations for change.

11: Customisers or conformers

Organisations differ because of the culture that has developed in each of them. Some show a preference for taking new ideas and then re-inventing them significantly. They will also take more risks and will often make a bid to be the first to get involved in a new project. These organisations can be referred to as '*customisers*'. On the other hand, some organisations would rather wait until others have demonstrated that the new practices work well, before they take up the challenge. They are called '*conformers*'. Neither is better than the other, they are just different ways of approaching new ideas.

"Neither a 'conformer' nor a 'customiser' is better than the other, they just have different ways of approaching and dealing with new ideas."

There are no hard and fast rules about determining who is a customiser and who is a conformer. However, you can look to the past activities of the organisation to get some idea of their preference. The advantage of making your thoughts explicit on this topic is that it can help you prioritise which group to work with first. It is no fun trying to get a large number of conforming organisations to be the first to adopt new ways of working!

There are many different ways to assess whether an organisation is ready for change. Unless you are conducting a research study in parallel to your rollout project, you will probably not need to use validated instruments.

12: Organisational readiness questionnaire

This tool provides you with a set of scales on a number of topics that are useful for carrying out your own, pragmatic, investigation. What matters is your analysis. There are no right or wrong answers.

A useful way to use this tool is to share your analysis with colleagues. Different people will have different points of view and discussing the topics and listening to the various opinions will help you understand more about the organisations with whom you are working.

13: Targeting individuals

When you get down to the detail of working with specific individuals, it is useful to consider whether they are more likely to try out your new ideas (*initiators*), whether they would prefer to wait until others have changed their working practice first (*majority*), or whether they prefer the status quo (*defenders*). What's important to recognise is that the same individual will adopt some ideas quickly and other very slowly. This tool guides you to think through whether the individuals you are working with are more likely to test out your ideas or not.

An alternative way of discovering where someone is in the acceptance of change process is to use this tool that is based on 'Prochaska and DiClemente's Stages of Change'.

14: Individual readiness for change

The value of this tool lies in the way you can segment your target audience and then work in different ways with them, depending on which stage they are at. The theory suggests people move from being *precontemplative* about change (they aren't even aware of the need to change), to *contemplative* (they are aware of the possibilities but haven't yet decided whether to have a go), to *action* (testing out new ideas) and then to *maintenance* (keeping going).

For those you diagnose to be *precontemplative*, you'll need to find ways to increase the tension for change. Help them to become aware of their own practice. Use benchmarking and audit to demonstrate that improvement is required.

The *contemplatives* need gentle attention and guidance. Small amounts of information and the opportunity to meet up with members of the pilot project team may help move them to action. If you identify some individuals who are ready for *action* then drop everything and work with them! They will get bored and disillusioned if they don't get the opportunity to make the changes when they want to make them.

"If you identify some individuals who are ready for action then drop everything and work with them!"

Later on in your project you'll be interested in the *maintenance* and *relapse* phases. It will be important to distinguish between the two and to diagnose what actions you could be taking to keep the new behaviours in maintenance and to avoid relapse. Each circumstance will be different. It's just important you recognise these are phases and you can influence how people move through them.

15: Stepping in their shoes

Before you set out on your first meeting, or in fact any interaction with potential adopters, it is worth spending a few moments looking at the issues from their perspective. In a busy project you can often become consumed with the need to deliver results and this drives you to focus on your tasks and activities. By considering the points of views of others you might find ways to break through resistance to change or even get new ideas on how the changes can be implemented. This tool will help you develop an empathy with your target adopters.

16: Identifying opinion leaders

Some individuals are more influential amongst their peers than others. This tool gives you some ideas how to identify these people and then find ways to support them so they can help spread your message and gain commitment to change in the organisations you are working with.

Tool 10: Drivers for change

Objective:

- List the reasons for an organisation to adopt new working practices

Task:

Decide whether you are working at the high level covering all your organisations or whether you are thinking about one organisation only.
List the reasons under the headings below.

Strategic and policy needs

Specific patient and carer demands

Technology issues

Workforce development issues and professional requirements

Financial demands

Hints and tips:

- Try and avoid general statements; give detailed descriptions. Be as specific as possible
- If you're unable to generate much of a list, then ask a colleague from the organisation you are thinking of to help you. It's essential you have some understanding of the drivers for change.

Tool 11: Customisers or conformers?

Objective:

- Discover which organisations prefer to either invent new solutions (*customisers*) or follow the actions of others (*conformers*)

Task:

List the organisations that are part of your rollout plan
Using your common sense, note which type you think each organisation is and why.
Make some notes on the implications of this for your rollout plan.

Organisation	Customiser	Conformer
•		
•		
•		
•		
•		
•		
•		
•		
e.g. Mainroad Hospital	*e.g. 1st wave Booked Admissions and developed bespoke IT system*	*e.g. Waited until the 4th wave Booked Admissions and then bought a ready made IT system*

Implications for the rollout plan:

Hints and tips:

- Your first thoughts are probably the best. There is no right or wrong answer
- Best if you don't try and do a detailed analysis
- Test out your results with colleagues. If they have a different view – discuss why.

Tool 12: Organisational readiness questionnaire

Objective:

- Assess the organisation against a number of key factors
- Summarise the implications of your results

Task:

Focus on the specific subject and task of your rollout plan.
Choose one organisation and mark your assessment on the table below.
Reflect on the results and make notes on the implications for your rollout plan.
Repeat the analysis for all your target organisations.

	High	High to Med	Med	Low
Overall impact on the organisation				
Costs of initial investment				
Magnitude of disruption				
How radical are the changes				
Certainty of good results and performance				
Status of the change in the organisation				
Amount of the organisation that will be affected				

Implications for the rollout plan:

Hints and tips:

- There is no right or wrong answer. Your first estimate will be fine
- Check your results with colleagues and discuss any differences of opinion
- When considering the implication, don't assume "low" answers are necessarily good! They could mean your project has very low awareness.

Tool 13: Targeting individuals

Objectives:

- Gain an understanding of your target audience
- Devise communication and change strategies that best suit your potential adopters

Task:

Write down the names of the individuals you need to work with to achieve your project rollout. These should be the people who will need to make the changes in practice. Reflect and make notes on how you might best approach them regarding your proposals.

Initiators	Majority	Defenders
First to implement the change. Often impulsive. Like to re-invent new ideas.	*Wait for others to change first. Need to see evidence the change works.*	*Have an interest in maintaining the status quo. Articulate concerns*
Names:	**Names:**	**Names:**
How to approach:	**How to approach:**	**How to approach:**

Hints and tips:

- Capture your early thoughts now, you can firm up your actions later
- If you don't know the names of your target adopters – then find out! It's important!

Tool 14: Individuals readiness to change

Objectives:

- Identify where individuals are in the stages of change
- Draw up plans to deal with the people in the different stages, differently

Task:

Write down the names of the individuals you need to work with to achieve your project rollout. These should be the people who will need to make the changes in practice. Reflect and make notes on how you might best approach them regarding your proposals.

Precontemplative	Contemplative	Action
Can't see the need for change. Not interested. Low awareness of ideas for change.	*Thinks some change is needed. Require information and evidence for possible solutions.*	*Wants to change. Wants to do it now.*
Names:	**Names:**	**Names:**
Action plan:	**Action plan:**	**Action plan:**

Hints and tips:

- **At a later stage in your project, repeat this exercise using *maintenance* and *relapse* as your criteria.**
- This is an alternative to Tool 13.
- If you have a group of individuals in a meeting, you could ask them to declare which stage they are at. This will help you customise your action plans and the way you can personalise the change programme to suit their needs.

Tool 15: Stepping in their shoes

Objective:

- Describe the issues from the *point of view of the adopter*.

Task:

Identify three different roles that are involved in adopting new ways of working
For each role, list some phrases that may represent their point of view
Reflect on the implications for your rollout project.

Role:	Role:	Role:
Issues: • • • • • •	**Issues:** • • • • • •	**Issues:** • • • • • •
Implications:	**Implications:**	**Implications:**

Hints and tips:

- Stereotypes are useful but you might like to avoid them where you can
- Use this tool if you perceive you have '*resistors*' to your proposals

Tool 16: Identifying opinion leaders

Objective:

- Identify opinion leaders and their views on your project
- Develop plans to support them

Task:

List 5 people who you feel are seen as influential by their peers and who you believe are important for the success of the project. Number the names 1 through to 5.
Assess these names against the questions
Note how you might best support the identified individuals

	Possibles				
	1	2	3	4	5
Demonstrates empathy; can see issues from differing perspectives					
Ability to deal with abstract concepts					
Ability to cope with uncertainty					
Evidence of ability to handle risk					
Displays aspirations to achieve and develop					
Networks outside own organisation and profession					
Exposure to and uses a variety of media/communication methods					
Knowledge of innovations, new and alternative practices					

Notes on how to support these opinion leaders:

Hints and tips:

- It is best to keep your assessment of opinion leaders informal. Calling someone a champion in public might mean they lose the credibility you were relying on!
- If you can't identify an opinion leader you may need to look outside the organisation you are targeting.
- Another way to discover opinion leaders is to ask those you are working with, "whose opinion do you value and respect on this issue?"

Section C

Mainstreaming activities

Heather sat with her head in her hands. It looked like all her hard work at Mainroad hospital was falling apart. As soon she turned her back things started to slip.

"The monthly data collection looks pretty simple. I don't know why they don't seem to have time to do it," said Richard.

"There was always resistance to collecting it, so I used to do it myself. I knew it was going to be an issue but I thought I'd managed to get agreement from the clinical nurse specialist that she would do it now."

"Have you asked her why she's not doing it?" enquired Richard.

Heather sighed. "I don't need to. I know all the excuses. *Not enough time, no use, not my job* etc. I also know all the stuff about making sure the work is embedded in the system if the results are going to be sustainable, but it's not that easy."

"I guess one of the issues with an innovative solution like the diabetes one is, that it is by definition, outside the norm. It's so unusual – and that is its success – that it makes it very difficult to become part of the normal everyday practice," declared Richard.

"Add to that all the small things that seem to keep changing that put the solution at risk. For instance, the general manager has sent out a memo saying all job roles have to fit within a certain grade. This means the clinical nurse specialist may need to drop some of her activities. Quite frankly, I don't feel confident it will last more than a year," said Heather.

"It's going to look a bit silly if we're trying to spread something that doesn't seem to be sustainable."

Heather countered, "I'm not sure that's the issue. I think the solution is sustainable; it's just the management and organisational stuff that seems not to be working.

"Maybe it's both the organisational issues AND the solution that have something to do with the sustainability issue?" suggested Richard.

"Somehow my project was never fully part of the organisation's day to day business. Innovation is one thing, but ultimately if the solution is to work then it will need to be part of the fabric of the hospital, not just the diabetes team."

"I think the term for that is *mainstreaming*," suggested Richard.

"More jargon," laughed Heather.

Richard stepped up to the white board and picked up a blue marker. "Ok, you tell me what you think the issues are and we'll see whether we can address any of this at the start of our rollout project. Off you go – call them out."

"Here we go:
- Senior managers in the organisation don't know about the project – I guess I never told them. I thought they might be put off by the fact we were coming up with innovative solutions in a very haphazard way
- That means I've no way of knowing whether the objectives of the project fit within the organisation wide aims and objectives, might help if they did.
- None of the other managers helped communicate what we were doing. Perhaps sharing good stories would have been useful to get their interest.
- I suppose I controlled too much of the project for too long. I should have ensured the clinical team owned it – except I was in the clinical team at the time; so that makes it complicated!

They reflected for a moment.

"It's an important list, Heather. Somehow, your experience is going to be valuable for the rollout stage. I can already see ways to involve senior managers at a very early stage in the project."

"Yes, I already want to change my project plan. I think it's worth spending more time in the early stages getting commitment and encouraging ownership," declared Heather.

"Mmmm. I suppose that means it will take longer to demonstrate results. Cathy might not like that," said Richard.

"Perhaps we should write up the notes you've taken on the board, list my learnings, come up with some recommendations and then send it to Cathy to mull over"

Mainstreaming; some introductory thoughts

Mainstreaming a project is crucial for sustainability. There are two factors to consider:

1. Involving the senior management of the organisation; the Top Team
2. Conducting the project in a way that doesn't create dependency on outside resources, such as the project manager.

> *"Conduct the project in a way that doesn't create dependency on outside resources."*

Engaging the Top Team in an organisation can be a challenging task. Tools 17 to 20 are all designed to help this process.

17: Top team checklist

Many Top Teams are aware of the pockets of innovative activity underway in parts of the organisation. However, when you come along in a rollout phase of a project, then it is worth spending some time providing them with some information about your aims and objectives, what the project is about and how it will impact the organisation. Don't assume they already know this. A small pack of information they can refer to is immensely helpful.

One issue for improvement projects is worth keeping in mind: measurement. Board members usually experience very high-level data and don't often get the chance to work with data expressly designed to measure improvements. Get your rollout team to work with a senior executive to explain how their measurements demonstrate improvement. This will raise issues of data collection and ongoing collection and management.

Encourage the senior executive to see if the measurements being used by the team could support other improvement objectives and goals in the organisation.

Top team support for your project is a key factor for mainstreaming and sustainability. You can't tell them how your project will contribute to their organisation. Instead, they need to work through what it means for them. They are the only ones who have the breadth of view to be able to see all the opportunities and impacts.

> *"Top team support for your project is a key factor for mainstreaming and sustainability."*

18: Integrating goals and objectives

This task can be done with the chief executive working alone, or directly with their team. The output should be updated at least once a year.

If there are a number of rollout projects happening in the same organisation at the same time, then you may wish to meet with your improvement colleagues and find a way to help the Top Team integrate all the activities into their organisational objectives and goals.

19: Top team communication

Many concepts and ideas that your team are implementing in their project may be applicable to other parts of the organisation. It's very helpful for the rollout team if there are ways to communicate not only what they are doing and why, but also their results and the impact they are having on the organisational goals.

Communication is key to any change process and any system needs to experience a large variety and large number of communication activities and events. Different professionals have different learning and 'hearing' styles so the more innovative and subtle the communication is, the more effective it will be over the longer term.

The project team will be managing a number of communication activities. A key role for the Top Team is to communicate the concepts, ideas, results and impact of the project work in ways that demonstrate how it is an integral part of the organisation. It's useful to share information through topics and agenda items other than the name of the project work. For example, instead of reporting on the "Access Project" it would be useful to highlight the impact of the project against one of your goals, namely, "Reducing waiting times".

The more the project and its results are discussed at all levels in the organisation, the more easily it will become part of everyday working. Communication from senior management and clinical staff will help raise the status of the change and credibility of the solution and the staff involved. The clinical team will then want to maintain the performance and if anything changes, there will be enough people who know about the project to be able to help them find new ways around any new problems.

20: Developing the top team script

Your rollout project, like many others, is wrapped up in its own jargon and most of the supporting material is written with a very specific focus in mind. You may find it useful to encourage the chief executive and other influential members of staff to spend a few minutes making some notes on how they might explain the work of this project, its potential impact and value to the organisation. Their own words and style are an important factor in organisational communication so translating the formal documentation into something more relevant to staff is an important step.

Tools 21 to 23 provide you with some ways to consider **reducing dependency of the project resources**.

Ownership is something that is taken, that is accepted. You can't give someone ownership. You can, however, conduct your project in such a way as to consciously influence dependency and ownership.

21: Designing ownership

The tension here is between your control over the project, driven by the need to demonstrate results, and the clinical teams' ownership of the activities, usually hindered by their perceived lack of resources and skills. There is no easy or quick fix. The trick is to make the issue explicit, and through discussion, find ways over time to shift the balance from your control to their ownership.

"Find ways over time to shift the balance from your control to their ownership."

22: Encouraging ownership

You need to encourage ownership so that everyone is ready to take on new responsibilities and activities at the same time. A useful task for you is to determine who is ready, willing and able, to work with them and encourage them to accept ownership. Equally, it's helpful if you can work out whether the lack of acceptance of ownership is due to someone being unwilling, or whether they lack the skills or resources – they are unable. This tool uses a *willing/able* framework to support your diagnosis and action planning.

23: Project manager assessment

Control is a personal issue. This tool starts you thinking about your impact and role in the project and how you may be helping or hindering the development of ownership by the local team.

Tool 17: Top team checklist

Objective:

- Develop the package for the Top Teams describing the rollout project and specifically the actions underway in their organisations

Task:

Collect and write materials that you can use to explain the project to the Top Team Use this checklist as the basis. Add more information if you think appropriate

❑ **Goals of the overall programme**

Your team is participating in a change programme called:....
Sponsored / funded by ...
Supported by ...
The overall goals of this programme are ...

❑ **Key dates, milestones and outcomes**

The following list provides you with a guide of what to expect when, from your team and from the programme as a whole...

❑ **Baseline data for your organisation**

Measurement is a critical part of this change programme; without it we would not be able to demonstrate improvements. When your team started their project they performed some baseline monitoring. They use this to assess their progress in making changes that are real improvements. This information is also used to monitor progress of the change programme as a whole.

The baseline information for your organisation is enclosed, and it is shown in comparison to the other organisation participating in this rollout project...

❑ **Specific goals and objectives of the organisation's project team**

Achieving these objectives is important to your team. Knowing about these and finding ways to support your team in the change process will be crucial for success. Enclosed are the objectives for your organisation's team...

Hints and tips:

- Keep the information pack short and to the minimum
- Involve the organisation team in writing the pack
- You can have one pack for all organisations, a master, and then just edit to customise for each organisation
- You should be able to develop this pack within a couple of hours...

Tool 18: Integrating goals and objectives

Objectives:

- Match rollout project objectives with organisational objectives
- Identify ways in which the rollout project contributes to the organisation

Task:

Ask Top Team members to complete the following. They enter their organisation's goals or objectives in the left hand column

Goals/objectives	This rollout programme supports this goal in the following ways:

Hints and tips:

- Look for organisation objectives that the rollout project contributes to that are not initially obvious e.g. workforce planning and development
- Different members of the top team may have different points of view. Ask them each to complete the form first, then summarise.
- This forms the basis for useful discussion with Top Teams or as a way to introduce yourself and your project to the Chief Executive

Tool 19: Top team communication

Objective:

- Develop a plan for raising awareness and communicating project results
- Move beyond the usual communication methods and try some more innovative approaches

Task:

List existing methods of communication within the organisation that can be used (e.g. newsletters, meetings…)
Brainstorm ideas for more innovative approaches in addition to using the above

(a) Existing methods of communication

(b) Ideas for new ways of communicating about this project

Hints and tips:

- Keep the new ways simple and achievable
- Some existing communication may not be obvious; think laterally!

Tool 20: Developing the top team script

Objective:

* Chief Executives to develop, in longhand their own script about this project

Task:

After explanation about the project, write up the following:

This programme is about.....

It is important for us because it ....

The advantages of this work are......

I expect the impact to be......

We can support our project team by.....

Hints and tips:

* This may not make sense to you or the rollout project manager; it is a personal piece of communication for specific circumstances
* Each member of the Top Team could do with developing their own script

Tool 21: Designing ownership

Objectives:

- Make explicit who is controlling vs. owning parts of the rollout project
- Design when to reduce control and encourage organisation to own the rollout project

Task:

List the activities and tasks that you own in the left hand column.
List those the organisation *should* own in the right hand column
Highlight those in the right hand column that the organisation does not yet own
Highlight the tasks you own that you would like them to own

I control...	They own...
•	•
•	•
•	•
•	•
•	•
•	•
•	•
•	•
•	•
•	•
•	•

Hints and tips:

- Tool 22 will help you encourage ownership
- There is no definitive list; just capture your thoughts and don't forget the second part of the task which is to do the highlighting in both columns.

Tool 22: Encouraging ownership

Objective:

- Identify who should be able to take on what tasks
- Develop plans to delegate and encourage others to carry out project tasks

Task:

List names of target adopters in the organisation who are willing (want to do it) or not, and who are able (have the expertise and resources) or not.
Make some notes on what action you need to take to start the ownership ball rolling

Willing and able	**Unwilling and able**
Actions:	Actions:
Willing and unable	**Unwilling and unable**
Actions:	Actions:

(adapted from Hersey & Blanchard, 1988)

Hints and tips:

- Capture your early thoughts now, you can firm up your actions later

Tool 23: Project manager assessment

Objective:

- Self assess project manager's ability to manage without full control of the rollout project

Task:

Answer the questions. Reflect and make notes on what you need to action.

If you were not at work this week, what wouldn't get done?

What activities do you enjoy most in this project?

Could some of these be carried out by others in the target organisation?

What plans are in place to either stop some of the administration (e.g. data collection) or carry it on after the project is officially complete? How can you avoid this being an issue at the end of the project?

What will make you most anxious if you have to give up control of it? Why?

Who is demanding control from you in a way that is hindering you encouraging ownership by others? What can you do about this?

Hints and tips:

- Be honest. There are no right or wrong answers.
- Your answers will depend very much on what stage you are in your project. If you are more than half way then be constructively critical about your approach.

Section D

Planning

"You promised me earlier that you would help me with the project planning," said Heather. "The paper work I have been given is filled with management gobbledegook. I thought milestones were those ancient stones alongside the main roads in England saying how many miles to the next place!"

"Well, project milestones are no different," explained Richard. "They are just pointers in your plan where certain things are expected at specific points in time."

Cathy, more concerned with getting the whole rollout programme off the ground with a flying start, dumped a pile of job descriptions and budgets on the table in front of Heather and Richard. "Before you get into the minutiae again, we need to work out how we are going to co-ordinate all the various projects going on in different organisations."

"Why can't the projects just be left to get on with their own work?" asked Heather. "They've got their own targets and plan."

"We need to have some idea what is going on – as a minimum, those who've put up the funding for the programme will want monthly status reports from us."

Richard and Heather both grimaced.

"I would have thought the most useful thing about coordination would be helping the different organisations to access information and to network with each other. The more they can help themselves, the easier it will be for us," declared Richard.

"Hey – that's our Richard – if there's a short cut he'll find it!" laughed Heather.

"Yup, I'm going to write the guide called "The lazy project manager's guide to rolling out projects!"

"Come on guys. Infrastructure. What do we need and how are we going to set it up?" asked Cathy.

Richard, remembering Cathy's previous concern about their comments on her programme plan, thoughtfully asked her whether she had already developed a strategy that they could work on.

"No, I haven't had time. I just made up some lines in a budget and thought we could thrash out the details nearer the time. And that time is now."

"Well, we could start with a bit more office space for ourselves, a laptop each and some administrative support," declared Heather.

Sensing Cathy wasn't impressed by this, Richard stepped in and added to Heather's ideas. "Of course, we'd be out and about a lot of the time, and having access to email whilst we travel would help us to be efficient. Come to think of it, we could host some chat groups on the web with the project teams."

"As you know, I'd prefer to meet with people face to face rather than over the email, so can we also find ways to have meetings? Is there budget for this?" asked Heather.

Cathy checked the spreadsheet. "Yes, well... There's an amount set aside for communication and that will also have to cover newsletters, the annual conference as well as any telephone conference calls we might set up."

"What about locum cover for the meetings and conferences?" asked Richard.

"I'd prefer not to pay for that," said Cathy, "the organisations need to do this work anyway and I don't see why they should have extra resource payment to cover it."

"That's a bit harsh," said Heather. "If there wasn't locum cover available for me when I was doing the pilot project, we'd never have even got started. It's not about incentive – it's just being practical."

"I see you point of view. Maybe there's a compromise here," suggested Cathy.

Richard thought for a moment. "How about providing each organisation with some project implementation resource and let them choose whether they wish to employ a person part or full time to work with them, or use the money to free them up using locums."

"Ok, let's cost that out," said Cathy. " Can you both draw up some plans on the communication processes we need, estimate the costs for meetings, the people resource requirements as well as any equipment. You need to take into account the project milestones and show how the money will be used in each quarter of the year."

"What about the cost involving in actually making the changes? Some organisations may need to reorganise the waiting room areas, for instance," said Heather.

"No, that's their costs. We're just looking at the infrastructure we need to set up. Can you also let me have your detailed project plans by the end of the week," demanded Cathy.

Mainstreaming; some introductory thoughts

This section brings together many of the areas you have covered in previous chapters and helps you work through ways to plan your rollout project.

Starting with **infrastructure**, you need to work out what is required to underpin the rollout. This covers administration as well as the way the various organisational project teams will work together, share information and learn from each other.

24: Infrastrucure checklist

You'll need to design an infrastructure that supports your programme in a way that makes the best use of the resources you have
to hand. Each situation will be different and there is no set way to
do this. This tool will help you to think through what pieces of
infrastructure you may need for your rollout project.

25: Milestones

Your project plan should begin with an understanding of the key
milestones. After that you can detail the various activities, who
will carry them out and when.

26: Timing

You need to pay careful attention to timing, to ensure you have
taken into account the amount of elapsed time that might be necessary to get all the right things in place for the changes to be
implemented efficiently. (See Tools 5, 6 and 7 for more guidance
on this.)

"Ensure you have taken into account the amount of elapsed time that might be necessary to get all the right things in place."

One of the traditional planning tools to show how the various
activities fit together over time, is the Gantt chart (see appendix).
You can draw up one of these quite easily by putting the months
across the top of your page, the activities down the side (rows) and
then drawing lines across the page, under the months, next to
each activity, to signify when the task will be carried out. You can
write on it the name of the person responsible. It's also a good idea
to mark your milestones on this timing plan.

It is easy to get carried away in the action phase and to start
testing changes that are not directly linked to your project aims
and objectives. Unless you have a specific reason for doing this,
you need to demonstrate how each of the project team's actions
are focused on delivering a specific aim or objective.

27: Linking actions to aims

This tool is a simple matrix where you verify that your actions are
linked to at least one (usually more) of the aims and objectives of
your project. It is useful to keep this list as a running action plan
for the project. Each organisational team should keep one,

especially if they are testing and implementing small scale changes where it is easy to get distracted and to start making changes that are not focused on delivering the project.

28: Communications framework

A communications plan needs to be dynamic and it helps to put in place a number of ways to generate feedback on your progress. Your plan needs to work at a number of levels and, where possible, involve communication activities outside the direct system within which you are working.

Tool 24: Infrastructure checklist

Objectives:

- Describe what you need in the way of infrastructure
- Work through how it fits together

Task:

Capture any additional infrastructure you think you need in the first column.
Make notes about availability or issues in the second column.
Reflect on the pieces and think through how it might all string together for your project.

Infrastructure examples	Notes:
Hard ✓ Office space/location ✓ Equipment ✓ Web site resource ✓ Knowledge base, information ✓ ✓ ✓	
People ✓ Project manager ✓ Administration support ✓ Technical, change methodology support ✓ Clinical support ✓ ✓ ✓	
Variable ✓ Meetings ✓ Conference calls ✓ Newsletters ✓ Conferences ✓ ✓ ✓	

Hints and tips:

- Capture your early thoughts now, you can firm up your actions later

Tool 25: Milestones

Objectives:

- List the key outputs required at specific dates in your project
- Assess the implications of these critical events

Task:

List the outputs and the dates due.
Reflect and make notes on what this might mean for your rollout plans.

Milestone	Due date

Implications for rollout plans:

Hints and tips:

- *Your project should have around 3–9 major milestones.* Any more, then you are probably capturing too many smaller ones. Go for the high level, big impact events and outputs.
- If the dates are not known, then note down your best guess.

Tool 26: Timing

Objective:

- Develop a project plan that reflects non-linear progress

Task:

List the outputs or what you expect to have progressed in each of the four sections (i.e. in each quarter of your project).

Section 1: 5% of total output
Section 2: 20% of total output
Section 3: 50% of total output
Section 4: 25% of total output

Hints and tips:

- Divide your project length into four. Each section is a quarter of your *total project length* (though the outputs, the things you deliver, will not fall into equal amounts)
- An output can be a measured achievement e.g. 20% reduction in cancelled appointments, or as products, e.g. clinical pathway written up, or as a description of activities such as a mapped process.

Tool 27: Linking actions to aims

Objective:

- Maintain focus of change activities on the project aims

Task:

List your project aims or objectives. Give each one a number.
List your current project actions or small scale changes and tick which aim or objective they are working towards delivering.

No:	Aim or objective
1	
2	
3	
4	
5	
6	

Actions underway	1	2	3	4	5	6

Hints and tips:

- This may be useful to keep as a working document, updated frequently by recording all small scale changes tested or implemented as part of your project.

Tool 28: Communication framework

Objective:

- Develop a plan for raising awareness and communicating project results
- Move beyond the usual communication methods and try some more innovative approaches

Task:

Enter the next 4 months in the first column
Note what methods of communication you plan to use in each month.
Aim for at least 5 activities per month.

Month	General publications	Personal touch	Interactive activities	Public events	Face-to-face
e.g.	*Flyers* *Newsletters* *Videos* *Articles* *Posters*	*Letters* *Cards* *Postcards*	*Telephone* *Email* *Visits* *Seminars* *Learning sets*	*Road shows* *Conferences* *Mass meetings*	*One-to-one* *Mentoring* *Shadowing*

Hints and tips:

- Go for variety every month

Section E

Sustaining progress

"How was paternity leave," enquired Heather.

"Paternity leave was great – but I've come back to a real mess," said Richard, despondently. "Three of my project team seemed to have gone backwards in the six weeks I was away. Not just stopped work, but actually regressed!"

"Gosh, mine are ok," declared Heather.

"Well, lucky you," said Richard, dumping his briefcase on his desk. "I must have got the difficult organisations."

"Not necessarily," explained Heather. "I think they're evenly matched."

"Sounds like a competition."

"Well, it isn't. Not for me anyway," said Heather, walking out of the office. She closed the door behind her.

Richard took out his monthly performance reports and tried to make some sense of what was going on. He had plenty of data. Various graphs showed how the results had been dropping off at three of the organisations. He pencilled a ring around two of the results. The eraser broke off the top of the pencil as he chewed it. "Yuk," he said, and spat it out.

Startled by the ringing, he threw the pencil in the bin and looked for the phone buried beneath his papers.

"Oh, hi Cathy."

"Welcome back. How's it going," she enquired.

"Um, ok," he said, unconvincingly.

"You've spotted the problem then."

"Er, the slight drop in results?", asked Richard.

"Yes. Good old-fashioned relapse. As soon as the project manager's back is turned the whole thing collapses. I thought you'd done the mainstreaming work we discussed."

"I did work with the Top Team but perhaps it's early days and those efforts haven't paid off yet."

Heather slipped back behind her desk, trying not to look at Richard.

"Perhaps the solution isn't the right one for those organisation," suggested Richard.

"Could be. Though I expect that isn't the problem. You could check out how they've managed to implement the key concepts and if it seems those concepts aren't good enough then we'll have to get the creativity consultants in."

For the second time in ten minutes, Richard grimaced. He hated those cheerful guys who breezed in full of fun and happiness.

> Changing tack, Cathy asked, " What feedback systems do you have in place to monitor performance?"
>
> "Well, the usually data collection and reporting," he explained.
>
> " I suppose you're just going to have to make some visits, get stuck in and find out what's happening. Can you let me have your action plan by the end of the week please. See you at the programme meeting after lunch today. Bye"
>
> Heather felt sorry for Richard. She'd experienced relapse in the pilot project.
>
> "What feedback is the clinical team getting?" asked Heather.
>
> "These reports." Richard waved sheets of paper in the air.
>
> "I presume they get to see the results before you do."
>
> "Heavens, no. I wouldn't expect them to understand them."
>
> "So how do you expect them to know what's going on?" said Heather. "What I learnt in the pilot project was we needed to have the results as soon as possible. I wanted to know whether the changes we made had provided a measurable difference. I also wanted an opportunity to make some adjustments – some recovery – before the project manager got hold of me."
>
> "Oh," said Richard.

Sustaining progress; some introductory thoughts

It is critical that project teams receive feedback on how they are doing, directly. They don't want to hear it from the project manager or a senior manager in the organisation. Without a feedback system being in place it's difficult for teams to know how they are doing and whether the changes they are making are having a positive impact. Even when the project is complete, there needs to remain a way to continue this feedback.

"Project teams must receive feedback on how they are doing."

29: Close the loop

This tool takes you through some questions and helps you analyse whether you have appropriate and sufficient feedback systems in place to support sustainability of the improvements.

30: Measuring progress

There are at least four different types of measurements for improvement projects. This tool takes you though an analysis of your current measurements so you can check whether you need to adapt them after the project has ended. Measurements that are more outcome focused, will be much easier for the teams to assess whether they are holding the gains of the project. Specifically, you should stop any solution measurements by the end of the project.

Processes cannot improve infinitely. There is always a limit, often caused by outside factors impacting on the original project.

31: Limits to growth

This tool helps you work through what might be the reasons for the slowing down of improvement momentum.

32: Coping with relapse

Relapses will happen. The critical issue for you is to work out whether it is a real relapse or part of the normal swings in how the system normally behaves. The best way to check this is to display your results using statistical process control techniques. These will show you whether the relapse is true or not. Control charts use statistical analysis to display when a process is within or outside the norm. Your audit department should be able to help you with the calculations, or you could search out how to do the technique in basic statistical books or by searching the web.

"Relapses will happen."

There are many reasons for relapses and each situation will probably be quite unique. It is worth spending some time assessing just what is going on – or not going on. This tool provides you with some ideas to start your assessment. You could spend many weeks assessing the issues, or even just an hour or so. The most important thing is to spend a little time diagnosing what might be the issues, before you develop action plans to improve the situations. You may also find it useful to refer back to the Stepping in their shoes Tool (15).

Sustainability is more than just holding the initial gains. When the project ends, you need to have left the expectation that the improvements will be continuous.

33: Further re-invention

Further re-invention is a tool that assists you in analysing the extent to which your original solution has been implemented and to review what further re-invention needs to happen.

Weick & Sutcliffe (2001) suggest that highly reliable organisations are those that can continually adapt. These organisations are sensitive to the slight nuances in the system that may have long term adverse knock on impacts and are flexible, nimble and quick to respond to changing conditions.

34: Assessing adaptability

This tool contains a very short questionnaire that you can use to diagnose the extent to which the organisations you've been working with can adapt to ongoing demands. It is designed to be a catalyst for thought and discussion. The implications you come up with, and the actions you plan to take to reduce their negative impact, will differ for each organisational context with which you are working.

35: Letting go

"Take time and plan so you can manage your 'endings' properly."

Letting go is about taking a personal step back from the project and an assessment of your needs, fears and plans as the project ends. You will have played an important part in the rolling out of the original programme and the time has come for you to move on. The way in which you manage your endings (Bridges, 1991) is crucial not only to your personal development, but also to the sustainability of the projects you leave behind.

This guide has taken you through a set of tools to support you in rolling out your project. You probably haven't used them all, and certainly not all of them in the order in which they are presented in this book.

Continue to use the tools as a basis for developing your diagnostic skills and for holding constructive discussions about your project. You may also find them useful for non-project work, such as general management in your day-to-day operational role.

Tool 29: Close the loop

Objective:

- Assess feedback systems, provide impetus for continuous improvement

Task:

Answer the following questions, including your reflections on how you can improve the process of feedback to the clinical team.

Is data collection and measurement a management task with the results primarily for management reporting, or is it an action completed by members of the team as part of their learning process? What are the implications of your answer?

Is the person who does the work, the immediate receiver of the feedback? *(e.g. does the clinical nurse specialist receive feedback on the length of time it takes to get the results from a chest x-ray, within 1 week and without going via another person).* What can be implemented to provide this quick response to the most appropriate person?

What is the minimum feedback you can put in place to support the learning of the clinical team? In what way will it be something owned by them, rather than imposed by the project?

How do the individuals in the team learn about their performance at the moment? Is this sufficient? How can you build on this?

How is the feedback made visible to the team?

Hints and tips:

- These questions may be useful for discussion in project meetings early on in the rollout. They are easy to deal with when discussed with a colleague.
- Not all feedback needs to be in the form of numerical measurements; qualitative discussion is also quite appropriate.

Tool 30: Measuring progress

Objective:

- Assess the ability of the project measurements to indicate meaningful progress

Task:

Review your list of measurements.
Assess their type, using the matrix below, and make notes on how you think they could be developed, with sustainability in mind (i.e. increase the measurement of outcome).

Measuring clinical outcomes *(e.g. fewer adverse bleeding events for patients prescribed warfarin)*
Measuring project outcomes *(e.g. the % of patients prescribed aspirin)*
Proxy measurements *(e.g. the 3rd available appointment to see a GP, as measure of access)*
Solution measurement *(e.g. number of hospitals with a one-stop clinic for diagnosing patients suspected of lung cancer)*

Hints and tips:

- Capture your early thoughts now, you can firm up your actions later

Tool 31: Limits to growth

Objective:

- Diagnose why it appears that improvement efforts are slowing down

Task:

Reflect and answer the following questions.
Discuss your answers with colleagues.

Has a better solution to the problem emerged?

What changes outside the immediate system have taken place that may be hindering further progress? Think policy, professional guidelines, organisation.

Are the key concepts (Tool 4) still applicable? How can they be refined?

What are the views of opinion leaders (Tool 16) on your project and its topic area?

To what extent does the methodology you're using impact on progress? Can you describe different tactics that may encourage further adoption and re-invention?

Hints and tips:

- You can do this diagnosis on either one team or their ability to continuously improve, or you can look at all your teams involved in the rollout programme and review why some of them appear not to have maintained momentum.

Tool 32: Coping with relapse

Objectives:

- Explain why the relapse has occurred
- Identify ways to overcome issues that appear to prompt relapse

Task:

Confirm the relapse is actual and not just perceived.
List the reasons why you believe the relapse has occurred.
Make some notes on how you might counteract the reasons for relapse.

How do you know the relapse is not just part of the normal behaviour of the system?

Political and organisational issues:	Individual and social issues:	Technical and methodology issues:
•	•	•
•	•	•
•	•	•
•	•	•
Possible actions:	**Possible actions:**	**Possible actions:**

Hints and tips:

- If you don't know whether your relapse is part of the normal behaviour or not, then spend some time learning about statistical process control charts, and applying them in your work. A web search on the key words SPC INTRODUCTION will provide you with some basic information. Else ask your audit department for help.
- Keep asking why (up to five times) to get to the root of the problem.

Tool 33: Further re-invention

Objectives:

* Diagnose whether sufficient re-invention of the changes has taken place
* Determine action to take with teams not achieving the anticipated results

Task:

Answer the following questions. Reflect and discuss with your colleagues, especially the teams involved in implementing your project.

What % of the key concepts (Tool 4) has been implemented? To what extent has each concept been applied?

List the current problems in the project area that the key concepts appear not to cover?

Why do you think the solution as originally envisaged may no longer be appropriate for the adopting team?

What activities can you stop, expand, divide up, do more of or do less of?

What quick, brainstormed, ideas do you have to regenerate life, energy and fun back into the project?

Hints and tips:

* Capture your early thoughts now, you can firm up your actions later

Tool 34: Assessing adaptability

Objective:

- Investigate whether you think the organisation is capable of ongoing adaptation and improvement

Task:

Number your project sites 1 through 5 (use a separate piece of paper if you have more than 5). Assess these organisations or teams against the questions using the following:
A = Meets criteria, B = somewhat, C = a likely problem for sustainability
Reflect and make some notes on what this means for your project completion

	Organisations				
	1	2	3	4	5
Good communication connection networks within the organisation					
Senior managers and clinicians are well networked outside the organisation					
Leadership and team demonstrates ability to cope with uncertainty					
Evidence of ability to make small refinements to working practices, quickly					
Management style that enables small tests of change to take place					
Culture allows for small mistakes, considering them opportunities to learn					
There are no rigid rules and regulations concerning the solution					
A significant amount of re-invention of the solution has already taken place					

Notes on what this means for completing the project:
(i.e. what can be done to counter some of the potential difficulties)

Hints and tips:

- Capture your early thoughts now, you can firm up your actions later

Tool 35: Letting go

Objective:

* Develop a personal action plan for giving up control and involvement in the project

Task:

Answer the following questions. Reflect and then make notes on what actions you can take to help create your ending.

What have been my major successes in this project?

How can these be captured and shared? *(e.g. reports, papers, conference presentations)*

What is actually going to change for you when this project ends?

What and who will you miss most when the project ends?

How can I maintain the relationships I have developed and continue to expand my personal network?

You should expect some signs of grieving. Which of these have you already experienced, and how are you preparing for the others: denial, anger, exploration, resistance to change, commitment to the new work?

Hints and tips:

* You may like to carry out this analysis about half way through your project, as well as nearing the end of it.

Appendix

Example of a Gantt chart

	Week 1	Week 2	Week 3	Week 4	Week 5	Week 6	Week 7
Milestones							
Complete all preparation and planning		Tuesday					
Complete the process map						Friday	
Complete the report							Friday
Team meeting 1		Tuesday					
Team meeting 2							Monday
Tasks							
Select team	▓						
Define process		▓					
Map high level		George					
Assess main problem areas							
Map details				▓	▓		
Analyse					▓	▓	
Discuss, test							
Prepare report							Sally

Milestones:	The key dates
Tasks:	What needs to be done
Timescales:	Choose a timescale that suits your project best; days, weeks or months
Who:	You can write the name of the person responsible or the task in a box

Microsoft Project™:

If your project is a large and very complex one, then there may be a benefit in you investing your time learning how to use this.

Microsoft Excel™:

The example above was designed using Excel and it took only a few minutes. This is best for simple projects.

Annotated bibliography

Allen RE. "Winnie-the-Pooh on Management". Methuen: London. 1995
A serious topic made explicit in an engaging manner. Deals with many of the issues relevant to project managers, including, not taking oneself too seriously.

Atkinson P. "Creating culture change; strategies for success". Rushmere Wynne Ltd: UK. 1997
A comprehensive overview written in a style that makes it easy to dip in an out of various topics. Focusing more on the reassuringly familiar than the creatively new.

Bridges W. "Managing transitions; making the most of change" Nicholas Brearley Publishing: London. 1991
A must-have for any change agent and project manager. A practical guide to supporting others through the transitions required for change to be a constructive process.

Elwyn G, Greenhalgh P and Macfarlane F. "Groups; a guide to small group work in healthcare, management, education and research". Radcliffe Medical Press, 2001
Fully comprehensive, easy to negotiate, guide to small group work. Suitable for the beginner, it includes hints and tips for understanding and working with others in small groups. Highly recommended for improvement project leaders.

Fraser, SW. "Accelerating the spread of good practice; a workbook for healthcare" Kingsham Press: UK. 2002
Provides a more comprehensive summary and thoughts around the theory and practice of the spread of good ideas. It focuses more on the social systems of change than on the management process of project rollout.

Fritchie R and Leary M. "Resolving conflicts in organizations", Lemos & Crane: London. 1998
A very practical guide to managing difficult situations. Theory is nicely balanced with practical advice and activities. An essential read for any facilitator or project manager in healthcare.

Hart E and Bond M. "Action research for health and social care; a guide to practice". OUP: UK. 1995
A useful text if you are approaching your project as an action research type activity rather than a management task.

Martin P and Tate K. "Project Management Memory Jogger; a pocket guide for project teams". Goal/QPC: USA. 1997
Small ring bound book that covers all the basics of managing projects.

Rogers, E. "The Diffusion of Innovations" The Free Press: USA. 1995
This is one of the most influential books on how innovations diffuse. Covering the history of the research though to an updated view on the theories and insights, it will give you more detail than you would probably ever need. An essential read for the curious and theoretically inclined project manager.

Weaver RG and Farrell JD. "Managers as facilitators; a practical guide to getting work done in a changing workplace". Berrett-Koehler Publishers Inc: San Francisco. 1997
An excellent guidebook that provides practical suggestions backed up by theory. An essential read for the project manager who is really interested in the art of facilitating change and improvement.

Weick KE and Sutcliffe KM. "Managing the unexpected; assuring high performance in an age of complexity" Jossey Bass: San Francisco 2001
Essential reading for understanding how reliable organisations are those that can continually regenerate, renew an adapt. Although the topic of the book is not explicitly about sustainability, it gives an excellent analysis and view on maintaining good performance.

Wheeler DJ. "Understanding variation; the key to managing chaos". SPC Press: USA. 2000
An excellent introduction into statistical control charts – or process behaviour charts, as Wheeler calls them. Carefully explained and avoids overwhelming the reader with the statistical gymnastics and

instead, focuses on the benefits of analysis. Highly recommended for the curious improver.

Other references

Hersey, P., & Blanchard, K. (1988) Management of organisational behaviour: Utilizing human resources (5th ed.). Englewood Cliffs, NJ: Prentice-Hall

Prochaska, J and DiClemente, C (1984) The Transtheoretical Approach: Crossing Traditional Boundaries of Therapy, Daw-Jones Irwin.

Thor CG. "Designing feedback; performance measures for continuous improvement" Crisp Publications Inc: USA 1998